Gallery Books
Editor Peter Fallon
GIVEN LIGHT

Michael Coady
GIVEN LIGHT

Gallery Books

Given Light
is first published
simultaneously in paperback
and in a clothbound edition
on 26 November 2017.

The Gallery Press
Loughcrew
Oldcastle
County Meath
Ireland

www.gallerypress.com

All rights reserved. For permission
to reprint or broadcast this work,
write to The Gallery Press.

© Michael Coady 2017

ISBN 978 1 91133 730 0 *paperback*
      978 1 91133 731 7 *clothbound*

A CIP catalogue record for this book
is available from the British Library.

Given Light receives financial assistance
from the Arts Council.

Contents

First Snowfall *page* 11
A Sweet Bell Ringing 14
Aisling 19
A State of Light 20
   SRUTHÁN 20
   THE HAUNTING 21
   HARVEST HOME 22
Believers 23
Are You a Library? 24
Diana in the Tide 28
Catch of the Day at the River Suir Café 29
It All Depends 30
Dear Afterlife 33
The Blind Poet's Vision of Spring 38
Freeze-frame 39
Given Light 40
Holding the Fort 41
How Beautiful the Feet 44
Last Tryst 47
Mountain Lakes 48
News from the Sky 49
Litanies and Light 52
Sightings 55
Stitching 56
Palestrina and Amigo Holden of The Hill 57
The Jock 63
The Jupiter Epiphany 64
The Other Half 65
The Garden and the Scattering 72
Walking the Ground 73
A Joyful Haunting 76
Where or When 79
Where There Was None 81
Changelings 82
On the Eve of a Tree-felling 83
Benediction on the Sixteenth Day of May 87

Notes and Acknowledgements 93

Again and as always...
there are no questions more urgent
than the naïve ones.
— Wislawa Szymborska (1923-2012)
from 'The Turn of the Century',
translated by Joanna Trzeciak

You can't be in heaven and on earth at the same time.
— Sonny Rollins, jazz musician

*to the memory of
Liam Hogan (1926-2014),
teacher and friend*

∼

*Hence in a season of calm weather
  Though inland far we be
Our Souls have sight of that immortal sea
  Which brought us hither...*
— William Wordsworth,
'Ode: Intimations of Immortality from
Recollections of Early Childhood'

First Snowfall

Once upon sometime
before my First Communion year
a man across the way
beckoned me aside
and said one day —

*Look down, child,
look down
at my shoe.*

Years on I'd come to know
that his black shoes were polished
and re-polished every day.
He was a man who'd soldiered
on the Western Front
and never after could abide
the stain of mud
or sight of blood.

*Look down, boy.
Look down at my shoe!
Can you see the first specks there?
The snow is on the way. The sky
is full of it, I guarantee.*

I bent low towards the dark
lustre of shoe leather
but could find no sign
of something from on high
as yet unknown to me —

turned my face to look up
past his head, towards the sky,
and thought I felt something

like a chill teardrop
surprise my eye.

Then, after I'd turned
back to my play,
the sky began to fall
about my head and feet
and I knew for the first time
the astonishing effulgence
of descending snow

absolving every imperfection
of the world from our doorstep
to the gateway and beyond
as far off as high slopes
and cairn of Slievenamon.

Out of all my lost
and unlost nights and days
that transfigured scene
remains as real and irretrievable
as dream.

Where now
that child self,
outside of time, enchanted
by transforming light?

And where the boots,
the broken feet of men
who knew landscapes of mud,
obscenities of blood, barbed wire,
shellfire?

The snow
is still
descending

and abides
as snowfall
of the mind.

A Sweet Bell Ringing

at the National Museum, Collins Barracks

1

Stooping towards the case that holds
the Easter flag unfurled over the GPO
I see myself reflected in the glass
and out of that recalling
the image of a girl who's kin
dissolving and transposed

to a night in November 1915
when her father leads her on violin
into the song by Moore
telling of Lir's lonely daughter
at a Town Hall concert to send out
some Christmas comforts
to the Western Front.

A frail girl singing in a minor key,
Annie Coady sends her song into the dark
above the gathered heads and hearts
of a town beside the Suir —

When will that day star, mildly springing,
Warm our isle with peace and love?
When will heaven, its sweet bell ringing,
Call my spirit to the fields above?

2

By chance she's in a Dublin hospital
as Easter's terrible beauty breaks,
the family in Tipperary frantic

for news of her to counter rumour
of revolution, German invasion,
the city shelled.

When Maytime mopping up is done
with firing squad, quicklime, Frongoch,
Annie is well enough to be sent
back home to Tipperary, her illness
gone to ground until she's nineteen

and then forever taken
from her brother's arms —
as he, who'll be my father,
will be from mine
in years to come.

3

Here now and under glass,
mute eloquence of object:
the flag of the Republic
fashioned by the shirt maker

Mary Shannon in the co-operative
at Liberty Hall; on Connolly's orders
hoisted above the GPO
as Pearse proclaimed the words below,

taken by the British
when Easter Week seemed done,
then after fifty years returned
from the Imperial War Museum —

part torn but larger than imagined
and of a stronger weave,
Irish Republic lettered in white and orange
on a vibrant ground of emerald green.

A photograph beside it here
has a score of British officers
at ease with swagger sticks
and arrogance of empire
that outflanks the setting sun

posing with the rebel flag
in Sackville Street, on the plinth
of a new monument repudiating
behind their unseeing heads
the right of any man to fix a boundary
to the march of a nation.

There at Parnell's feet of bronze
imperial victors of the hour
frozen by the lens
in black and white
a century ago
look towards the unmade future,

brandishing insurgent green
in mock-ritual tableau
more prescient of what's to come
than they could know.

4

I am of that future
in the here and now that finds me
gazing through the glass
and all it gathers in around
the woven cloth displayed —

those dead imperial soldiers posing
live with Mary Shannon's flag
that survived all; the haunting
cadence of Moore's song
that tells of swan and star,
transfiguration, love,

and my father's sister Annie
long gone although still young
and smiling from the frame
by the doorway in our hall —

a little life unsung,
collateral to
the General Post Office,
the river Suir,
the Somme.

Aisling

The timbre of a voice
may say more than it says.
A woman on the radio

tells this morning's
weather news
in locally accented

words of deep simplicity;
complicit earth,
conspiring sky

conjuring a *spéirbhean* vision
from a time ouside
of time —

Spells of mist and drizzle
making way for sunshine
and light showers, with
some fog lingering a while
on hills and coastal parts . . .

Her voice
embodies
a *ceo draíochta* —

its strangeness and its distance,
its intimate
surprise.

A State of Light

*Each old is new
and every new is old.*

Connemara
is a state of light,
of wind and wild
and fluent sky —

flayed rock
and flowering bog,
storied lake and inlet
and deep song.

*Bíonn gach sean nua
is gach nua sean.*

SRUTHÁN

Beside a stream in Mámean
two lovers on a summer's day
surrender to dreamtime
of flowing water and lark song.

A pair of ravens lifts and loops in play
on thermals above Lough Inagh and Derryclare
while miles up in the blue
faint aero-trails skywrite
a kiss-cross sign
over the world.

Woman and man embrace
and share the gossip of the stream
and of the earth, sheep bleating
on the slope above,

a tractor with man and dog
trundling on a rough road below.

This is a time that's given
to the lovers of Mámean
and is eternal for as long
as its day lasts,
for no day ever
can return.

*Bíonn gach sean nua
is gach nua sean.*

THE HAUNTING

There is a solitude in every soul,
yet lovers go on loving
in the world's unending quest
for completion in the other,

but lost within the light of Connemara
there is a buried dark, a maw
of loneliness, an *uaigneas*,
a haunting from the years
of hunger and disease,
of coffin ships and horror
so unspeakable
that even as we reach out
to its appalling cries
we must allow ourselves
to turn aside
from death to life.

*Bíonn gach sean nua
is gach nua sean.*

HARVEST HOME

Season of ripeness
under twin spires of Clifden
that aspire beyond the mountains
and the stars.

The Muses bless the town
in the light of harvest home
proclaiming this a time
of festival and joy

and as its closing ritual
the young shape-shift and parade
through evening streets
en fête and astir

with drumbeat and dance
and a flourishing of lights
to face down once again
the chill nightfall —

for Connemara yet remains
a state of light,
of wind and wild
and fluent sky —

flayed rock
and flowering bog,
storied lake and inlet
and deep song.

*Bíonn gach sean nua
is gach nua sean.*

Believers

Your unbelief seems stronger than my faith
as though securely founded on a rock
from which you may believe with certainty
in some noGod, ineffably not there,
nor needing to exist or to explain —

and this becomes your clear theology,
one no more free of mystery
than my intuition's reach towards One
enfolding all beginning and all end.

We both acknowledge earth and sea and stars
and know both good and evil in the world,
the gravity and grace of love and grief —
all that is seen and all we cannot see,
over and under, beyond and between.

Are You a Library?

She is a small girl suddenly appearing one evening at my front window, wide-eyed behind her glasses, and calling out to me from the gathering dusk and shrubbery outside. I have already switched on the light inside my den, but forgotten to close the blinds.

The little girl seems mesmerized by the chanced-upon spectacle of this lit-up oul' fella on dramatic display amongst floor-to-ceiling bookshelves crammed to capacity.

'Hey Mister!' she calls out daringly again. 'Are you a library?'

It's only then I notice a second little girl standing to the side in the colluding half-dark, before the pair of them turn and scamper away, giggling, and leaving me with that arresting from-the-mouths-of-babes question hanging in the air: *Are you a library?*

Along with all the ordinary accoutrements of living our semi-d shelters some five thousand books; in my front-room den mainly, but also in the living room, bedrooms and overflowing into the attic. Domestic tensions and manoeuverings may be triggered by such biblio-clutter and colonization.

I've long since theoretically reached the stage of having run out of available space for new arrivals. Yet books still continue to sneak in and accumulate; new or second-hand, purchased or gifted. Sometimes they've been evicted in clear-outs of others' attics and turn up at my door pleading for refugee book status on the apparent basis that some people in my community do indeed believe that I maintain a handy book sanctuary...

I try to keep the lot catalogued and mapped in a computer programme which works well — so far. The whole technology of digital archiving remains untested in terms of ultimate durability — but that's another story. The internet is both a chaotic new world and an amazing phenomenon. I have used a computer as a writing and reference tool since the late nineteen eighties. I also own an e-reader which has its uses and convenience.

But the real book as we have known it and still know it is a core artefact of civilization. It remains unquestionably one of the greatest cultural, social and technological achievements of mankind across the ages.

A special part of my own collection is a bequest of books from an old friend and book collector, Hugh Ryan, who spent his entire working life as a humble assistant in a drapery store in Carrick-on-Suir, but whose lifelong passion was books, often rare or scarce first editions, some beautifully bound and in some instances signed or inscribed by their authors or former owners.

One remarkable example is a Latin Bible printed in Lyons in 1568, with bound and folded-in woodcuts and maps and handwritten marginal notes in Latin by a clergyman in the early 18th century. Most affecting and arresting of all for me perhaps is the inclusion in it of locks of some lost loved one's auburn hair — probably a girl's or woman's — unfaded by the centuries and pinned to particular scriptural passages . . .

In the great cosmic sweep of Sonnet 65, *Since brass nor stone nor earth nor boundless sea*, Shakespeare articulates despair at the relentless maw of time devouring everything and consigning it to the black hole of oblivion:

> *Oh how shall summer's honey breath hold out*
> *Against the wrackful siege of battering days*
> *When rocks impregnable are not so stout*
> *Nor gates of steel so strong, but time decays?*

But finally he pauses, with the quill pen poised above the page he writes upon, to sign off with this prophetic lifeline to the future:

> *. . . unless this miracle have might*
> *That in black ink my love may still shine bright.*

Story is all, and all is story. Each one of our unique individual identities is also linked existentially with a vast inherited catalogue of all the ghosts, known and unknown, encoded in our given database of genes; our incorporated inner libraries of lived-out human lives and the stories they engendered...

Books and manuscripted words carry us beyond frontiers of memory and archival record. They also draw us into mystery and enchantment, the parallel universe of the imagination, linking us with the souls of the living and the great multitudes of the dead. James Joyce rhetorically asked: *What is imagination?* And responded, *What is it but memory?*

And so the sheer delight of reading as a sustaining and interactive communion is a lifelong gift once triggered. We could scarcely afford books in my pre-television boyhood, but books were valued in our house, as was music and education and writing. Such was the given air we breathed, no matter how bare the cupboard. I was scarcely ten years old when I became incurably addicted through my fortuitous and life-changing discovery of Mark Twain and Huckleberry Finn, or R M Ballantyne, author of *The Coral Island* and *The Dog Crusoe*... along with poems I fell in love with and embraced by heart.

And so such innocent initiation and encounter from my childhood has led me on and delivers me back again to our semi-d that shelters a store of books and papers. And calls up again the apparition of that girl outside my window, like a lost child in a fairytale chancing on a lamplit cottage in the forest, standing on dark earth, but seeking out the light within; the word, the story...

Yes, little girl. I am a library.

And so, in your own unique way, are you.

And so is everyone.

LIBER ECC
SIASTICVS.

A ... illo fuit
& est ante æ-
um. Arenā ma-
quis & pluuiæ gu-
& dies sec...
quis dinumera-
uit? Altitudinem ...li, & latitudinem
terræ & profundu... byssi quis dimé-
sus est? Sapientiam ... præcedentem
omnia, quis inuestig... Prior omniū
creata est sapientia, & ...
dentiæ ab æuo. Fons sapientiæ ...
Dei in excelsis, & ingressus illius man-

nedicetur. Dile...
...ientia. Qui...
...diligunt e...
...agnali...
...nior
...tia ...
...
...
...scientia
dict, &
atque g...
num b...
tion...
...est, tim...
...ctibus illiu...
Implebit à ge...
...la à thesau...

Diana in the Tide

One evening by the river
a fisherman drew me aside,
gestured towards water, earth and sky
and parsed for me

his syntax of the tides,
the neaps, the springs,
and how the moon
was deeply implicated.

Walking on
in the conspiring dusk
it dawned on me
that deep down in his eyes

the fisherman implied
it was the river and the tides
that brought about
the moon's remaking.

I stopped to think on this
beside the dark floodtide,
saw the shaping goddess
wavering under water.

Catch of the Day at the River Suir Café

for Ralph O'Callaghan, 8 July 2011

Boatman, fisherman and friend,
mark the day that we were given
when you took me upriver
against fifteen miles of current
from Carrick to Clonmel.

Shades of boatmen in our blood
were with us and within us
by sun and shower and time,
by every weir and pool and bend,
to land the poem and story
called 'Going by Water'
telling of your father's
river funeral to a gathering,
with a party there to greet us
on the quayside, lead us
to the River Suir Café,
to the upper room and reading
for the men and women there.

So mark well then, my friend,
that day you took the helm,
as your fathers did before you,
and we cast off from Carrick
to go those miles by water
and later turned downstream
with farewells in the evening
having shared 'Going by Water'
with the living who'd assembled
in the town of *Cluain Gheal Meala*
at the River Suir Café.

It All Depends

Give greeting as you enter the butcher's this fine morning. The usual cutlets. Look on fearfully as always at the threat of lethal blade to Kevin's fingers as he cuts. Fourth generation in the trade under this slated roof in Lough Street. Talking expertly of Sunday's drawn hurling game. Missed chances. That point in the last seconds gone a bare inch wide of an All-Ireland victory. But younger Tipperary legs might yet prove fresher in the upcoming replay.

One hand steadying carcass of lamb, the other engaged with saw, with blade and cleaver. Time after time such intimate acquaintance between the living hands and blade each morning whetted. How finely may edge be honed before all edge is gone?

Behind all this an archaeology of inscribed scars criss-crossing butchers' blocks through generations. Did forefathers' fingers go unscathed? Cut after cut. Chances and near misses. Bleating and birthing of past seasons. *Little lamb who made thee?* Pasture land of Knocknaconnery out the road. Spurting blood in Cregg slaughterhouse. Friday the killing day.

Lamb. *Uan. Agnus.* Latin chant from altar or gallery all of his boyhood in the choir of the big chapel. *Agnus Dei, qui tollis peccata mundi.* Mrs Shelly at the organ. Bloody Sunday 1920, her husband-to-be Jerry Shelly on the Tipperary football team opposing Dublin in Croke Park. Auxies and Black and Tans invading the pitch, random volleys shaping history. Jerry risking all, running from midfield to retrieve a new overcoat from the sideline where already there are dead and dying. Blood congealing on green sward; priests kneeling by the stricken. Jerry snatches up the new coat he's borrowed that morning from his father. Gets home to Tipperary; lives to die another day in years to come.

And she who married him will live beyond a hundred. Her backlit silver hair set against spread pages lamplit in the organloft when you were a boy. High Mass or Benediction. Forty Hours' Adoration. The Divine Praises. Tremble of flooring boards within the organ loft. *Adoremus in Aeternum.* All-encompassing vibration filling sacred space, bespeaking mystery, while in itself a mystery. From high roof ridge and rigging of the nave down to the flooring of the aisles and ageless earth beneath.

Decline *agnus*, second declension. *Agnus agni agno agnum.* Chalky soutane of the teacher you remember in the school up on the hill. The pendulum clock, the weeping rain down classroom windows. Kindly man of Latin, maths and prayer.

This morning boys we'll plunge straight into the parabola.

His nickname. *Parabola.* Pupils reinvent their teachers. Custodian of beehives in the monastery orchard and passionate believer in Kilkenny hurling. Proclaiming all-time greats like Lory Meagher, the famed Lorenzo the Great of heroic solo run and dodge through all the field to net a legendary goal in 1935. A witnessed moment of perfection raising the hurler of Tullaroan to the teacher's classroom pantheon of Euclid and Pythagoras, Horace, Cicero and Virgil, Aogán Ó Rathaille and Shakespeare, his order's founder Edmund Rice of Callan and Rita of Cascia, patron saint of the impossible.

Parabola. That gaunt man of kindness, now years gone down the lonesome road; believer in a power beyond the possible. The pot of orchard honey he bestowed on you in recognition of your Leaving Cert results. The innocence and sweetness of that gesture from the long ago, returned to ambush ordinary now and here of Kevin, knife in hand, musing on replay and chance.

You can never be up to the Cats, though their best forward is in trouble since their last meeting-up with Limerick. Bad news, the torn hamstring, in either man or beast. But still you could never be up to them. The black and amber. Always ready with the lightning strike. Just when you least expect it.

He pauses with the knife in hand, looks up and shakes his head before again addressing the block to make the final cut.

I'd say it could be close in the finish.
It could be very close.
It all depends.

Dear Afterlife

i.m. Dennis O'Driscoll who died Christmas Eve 2012

Dennis, poet, man of letters,
I've unreasonable faith and hope
that you and I might still devise
between the lines
some ongoing intercom,
never mind that from now on
you'll persist in seeming
to sing dumb.

And so that's where I'm coming from
with this on-the-spot
account of your send-off —
some details you might wish to scan
for reference or even just for fun
assuming you can contrive to link
from that other side
to which you were so abruptly
snatched from Naas on Christmas Eve

around the very time that I
was following my wife
into a Kilkenny charity shop
where, while she felt her way
through racks of resale clothes,
I picked up for a song
three symphonies of Haydn
and a hardbound translation of
Rousseau's *Confessions*.

How strange — yet not strange at all
since life was in full swing —
that on that afternoon
while I played at being my own Santa Claus

in High Street, Kilkenny,
you were headed into mystery
of ultimate lift-off from
the general hospital of *Nás na Rí*,
leaving Julie beside herself
in untold shock and grief amid
tinsel, carols, Christmas trees,
that eve of the Nativity.

Remember then, after the feast,
on New Year's Eve
we walked you through the town,
a dozen or so poets to hand
forming an honour guard's embrace
both sides of the hearse,
under insinuating rain.

Back there in the church
we'd shared a deep communion
of love and loss (how good it was
to chant *Kyrie Eleison*). Whatever else,
we recognize the proper weight of death —
its drop to final deep beyond coastline
and continental shelf.

Standing there to speak for you,
Seamus, your friend,
the tousle-headed kerne, *saoi*
of Derry fields and byres and sheughs
as well as halls and towers of Academe.
Could he have had an inkling
of the shadow at his shoulder,
how, in mere months to come
he too would follow on the path
of no return?

See us shuffle on towards the graveyard
on that New Year's Eve. You may
have been surprised to note
(in cars, shop doorways or on footpaths)
how many men and women pause
to bless themselves as we pass by.
I salute their decency,
recalling words of Eudora Welty:
Every feeling waits upon its gesture.

A sign up front insists GET IN LANE —
something you could have devised
to put the wind up in us
no matter how we try to veer today,
tomorrow or next year —

and you're still showing us the score
when towards the edge of town
the hearse driver signals a left turn
into St Corban's place of graves
where, to the side, another sign
reads LOW HEADROOM.

At this point we of the honour guard
in moving on take a wrong turn
and briefly lose contact
with the whole cortège.
But see — there it is upon another path
and with as much aplomb
as can be faked the confused bards accelerate,
short-cut across the uncomplaining dead,
coming in first at the finish line of open grave
until you and the rest arrive.

Final rituals then are seen to and intoned,
we chant *Salve Regina*
and one way or another
you're home and dried.

I share this melancholy reportage with you
and with posterity
because at heart we're story tellers
to one another in this world, instinctively
including in our tellings those
who've gone beyond
the firelit circle of the living.

The gravediggers stand by,
waiting to close earth's open
mouth again and tidy up.
Theirs is a job that gets
into the pores, and to the core.
They'll spruce up later on,
head out on the town
to bid farewell to the old year
and see the new one in.

Nothing for it then but leave you there
and drift away, bypassing the signs
for GET IN LANE and LOW HEADROOM
this darkening afternoon.

In Lawlors Hotel hot whiskeys
are the order of the day
and there before us is a cluster
of army officers in dress uniform,
their unbuckled swords ranked
by the wood fire; reflected flame
dancing on steel.

Has there been some kind of *coup d'état*
at the Curragh while we were off guard?

Nothing so dramatic, Dennis:
no sooner were you carried from the church
than an army wedding party
was warming up to enter. This is
the exquisite heart-rending liaison
and flame of life and love and death —

on this last dying day of the old year
bride and groom make of this inn
an everywhere of time and space
with fire and funeral.

And so we eat and drink and gossip on.
I raise a glass that is still warm,
propose a health embracing
both sides of the dark river —

be with us, poet, in our liaison —
Sláinte na mbeo is na marbh.

The Blind Poet's Vision of Spring

from the Irish of Anthony Raftery (c.1784-1835)

With the coming of spring the light will be gaining,
so after Bríd's feast day I'll set my course —
since it entered my head I'll never rest easy
till I'm landed again in the heart of Mayo.
I'll spend my first night in the town of Claremorris
and in Bal' I'll raise my glass in a toast,
to Kiltimagh then, I could linger a month there
within easy reach of Ballinamore.

I testify here that the heart in me rises
like a fresh breeze lifting fog from the slopes
when I think on Carra and Gallen below it,
on *Sceathach a' Mhíle* or the plains of Mayo.
Killedan's a place where all good things flourish,
blackberries, raspberries, treats by the score,
were I to stand there again with my people
age would fall from me and I'd be restored.

Freeze-frame

On the night the stranger landed
from far off Butte, Montana,
he hired a hackney and pub-crawled
three townlands until, like a gunman

in a B-movie Western,
he pushed in the door
of The Cosy Thatch, lurched into
the light and silenced all with

*Would any of the Ryans
buried in* Cill an Easpaig
*please stand up
to be counted?*

A freeze-frame deep as lifetimes
held out for some seconds
against the TV in the corner
and noises from the yard

until two hesitating women
and an old man holding cards
stood up to turn and face
the stranger's outstretched hand.

Given Light

The moon hangs there as though that setting
and that space between the trees
had always been intended to receive it —
those two trees I planted years ago
on a day that I remember for the urgent
press of spring informing earth and air,
my daughter playing beside me on the grass,
the ache of limbs after digging and planting —

such a day of seeded consequence . . .
never imagining that on this particular
night of my own future I'll step out
from my house into the dark and there
be ambushed by the moon this moment ripe
between the silhouetted birch and ash,
each tree just as I positioned it that day,
but now grown many times my stature.

Unearthly radiance here discloses
all things as one but individual: roots
embracing and embraced by clay, communing
vitally with leaf and branch and dreaming bird,
beneath the moon in its cold orbit framed,
held for a moment in the lucent space
presented there between live plantings.
How perfectly the parts seem to fit

as though designed for this, along with
all else implicit and complicit in the frame,
such as this older self rooted in surprise
here now on moonstruck Earth, breathing my share
of its slim envelope of air while heart
beats out its little time under this light
where others I have known are gone ahead
into a radiance or dark that's absolute.

Holding the Fort

Leenan Fort in tandem with Dunree Fort protected the safe haven of Lough Swilly. The fort is now in a terminal state of decay.

By the time I happen
to be here above Lough Swilly
on this June day
history's ghosts
are gone with the wind
or underneath the waves,

the sea's face unmarked, as always,
by human time or happening
and Leenan Fort, well grounded,
continues to surrender
unconditionally
to terminal decay —

which is to say a flowering,
where grass and heather, lichen
and wild flowers colonize
cutstone blocks of gun emplacements
and imperial metal mountings
that rust and morph to burnt umber,
leaching back into the clay.

On nights of wind and rain
sheep shelter in the tunnels,
empty chambers
of decommissioned magazines.
Last orders have been shouted here,
last flags lowered and furled;
all ranks reassigned
to what are or will prove to be
their final postings
under earth or under wave.

It happens that I happen
to be here alive this June,
this year, this day,

as skylarks hover,
hold the fort in ageless
colloquy of earth and air
with grasshoppers below them
which chirp their own ground-level
terms of courtship
to a tune

that's stood them in good stead
since the early Triassic —
200 million or so
years ago,
it's said.

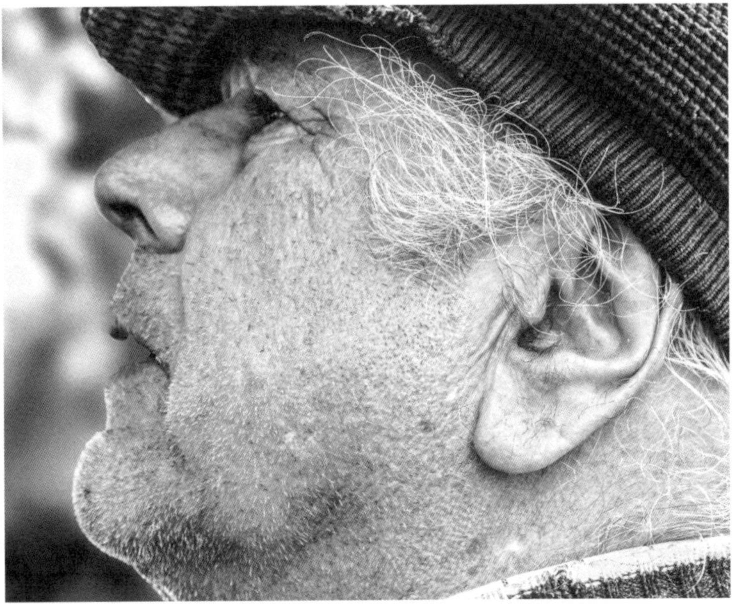

How Beautiful the Feet

We stop for directions
at a crossroads
and a church

just as service for
Remembrance Sunday
closes

and all the verses
of *Abide With Me*
are done.

Look how those living
men and women
linger there between the trees

around the church
to greet and chatter
as though that was all

there was or is
to all of this —
and meanwhile

see, oh see,
how beautiful
the feet

of their small children
playing hide and seek
among headstones

in morning sun that highlights
last night's frost
on grass and leaves,

on carved and lichened names
of father, mother,
daughter, son —

the word belovèd
sidelit in stone.

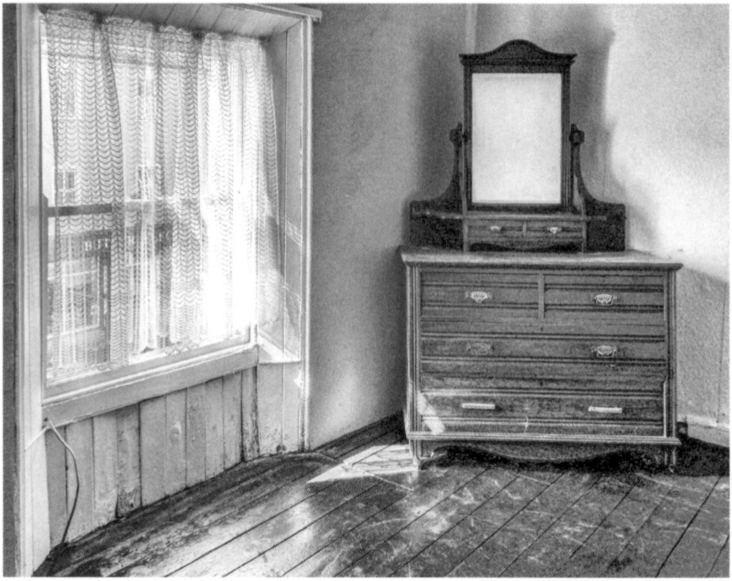

Last Tryst

After she's showered
she stands before the glass
to make up her face,

adjusts her hair
and earrings,
applies a rose lipstick —

the kind that boasts
of perfect pout,
hydrating shine.

She puts on dark coat
and gloves, then opens
the front door

to face
the morning world,
the raw east wind,

the taxi waiting
by the gate
to take her in

to where she'll walk
behind the wife,
the next of kin

holding in her heart
what was,
what might have been.

Mountain Lakes

Fed by glaciers long ages
before footfall or first fire

those Comeragh lakes
in which I used to fish

but can no longer reach —
more than ever now

they deepen in my mind
as I live on and breathe

below them in this pastoral
south Tipperary valley.

Never was the lakes'
high hauntedness

so much with me
as now, for since

I can't climb to the lakes
they often come to me —

their unseen mists
by night descending

to infiltrate the timeless
realm of dream.

News from the Sky

Switch off the clamour and take
the path by the river. There's Teresa
before you, face turned up
to the sky from her wheelchair.

*They're back this last week. Isn't it
a wonder to God how they can
make it all that way every year?*

Follow her eyes, take in aerobatics
this given evening between
the river and Poorhouse Field.

*And even to the same nests if they're
still there. The old people used to say,
Evict a swallow and your cow goes dry.*

'Helpless, downy' they enter the world,
says the guide. We're helpless too —

our coming and leaving
utterly bare.

Hirondelle, fáinleog, la golondrina,
outflanker
of winter

and over-flyer
of all human
history.

AH
STOP
P.J
Callain
CALLAN
SOCIAL.
DANCING
THE AULD
HOUSE
KILLAMERY.
EVERY FRIDAY.
NIGHT

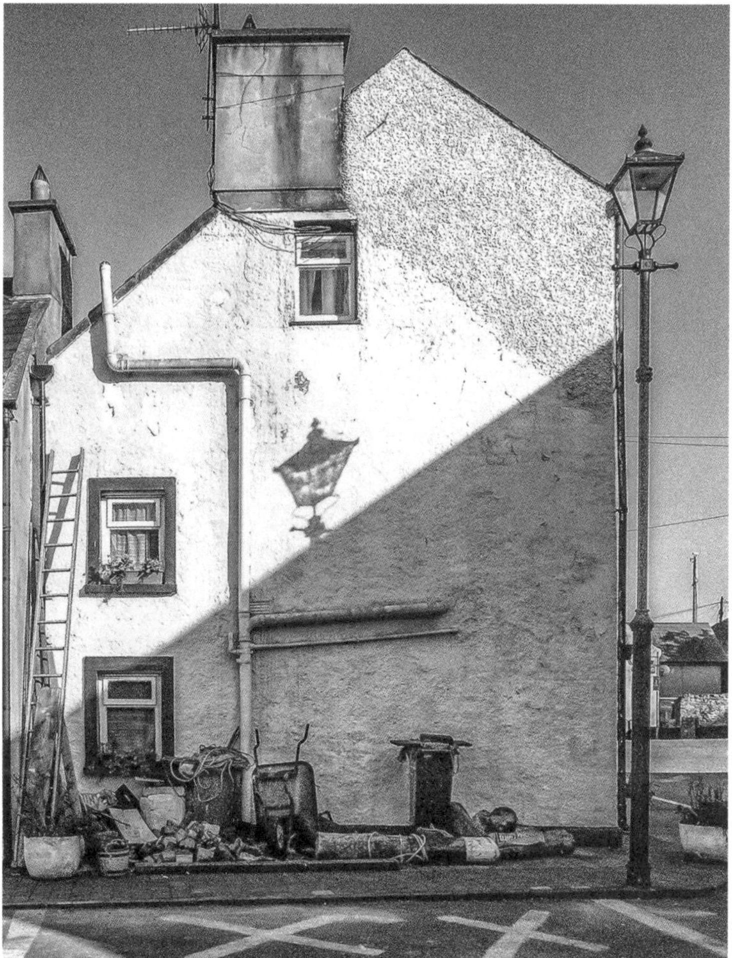

Litanies and Light

After food and wine
we drift outside
to the night garden,
unveil the telescope,
take turns to find
the lunar landscape,

while in a crowded house
a field and farmyard away
there is another gathering:

an old woman
is dying, has been dying
for a week,
pillowed in her townland's
intricate nest of kinship
and acquaintance.

Out there we find
a blinding pool of light
until the lens defines
an oblique horizon,
a freeze-frame of moonscape
in surreal counterpoint.

Kin have gathered
for the old woman's going;
tonight they've all processed
into the room
to say goodbye

with the mystical
matter-of-factness
of Irish country people,

touching her hands and forehead,
reassuring her one by one
as though this journey
were like any other
of her life,
its days and nights.

Out there,
remote and regal,

Sinus Iridum
Mare Frigoris
Lacus Somniorum
Mare Foecunditatis

mountains,
plains and valleys
of utter mystery
and silence.

The old woman
slips lightly
in and out
of being.

Faces she has known
orbit distantly
about her
in the room.

She'll go soon.

They pray,
make tea

and pray again
to the Virgin Mary.

We invoke the moon across the fields.

Sea of Tranquility
 Tower of Ivory
Bay of Rainbows
 House of Gold
Sea of Fertility
 Mystical Rose
Lake of Dreams
 Mirror of Justice
Sea of Serenity
 Morning Star
Sea of Nectar
 Gate of Heaven . . .

Sightings

Do you believe
in love at first sight?
I asked a woman,
to see what she'd say.

Love at first sight?
Oh yes, there is
such a thing,
she said —

but it mightn't
begin
just there
and then.

And can it go on
through the days
and the years
until death intervenes?

Then it's love
at last sight,
I suppose
you could say —

no one knows
what that weighs
till they meet it
someday.

Stitching

for Patrick and Clementine, safe delivered, Spring 2016

She's stitching coverlets
of found patches,

bits and pieces
from her life

to shelter infants
nestled in the wombs

of each of her
two daughters

who once nestled
in her own.

Palestrina and Amigo Holden of The Hill

The imperfect is our paradise.
— Wallace Stevens, 'The Poems of Our Climate'

1

There was that first time ever you heard of the man and the music he composed. Palestrina and polyphony; High Renaissance and all that. Like some shining revelation at the time. You were fairly well versed already in Gregorian chant. And love it still. But that too is banished from most churches now in favour of the banal and the happy clappy.

But back to that day as a student, in a college chapel and suddenly transfixed by the sound of a choir rehearsing, *a cappella,* taking you by surprise from behind and overhead. A sound like nothing you'd ever heard or known about before until then. A sense of glory dawning; a lifting off the earth.

Perhaps that effulgent sound could be what 'God' and 'Heaven' and all the rest of it might be about? A motet by some long-dead person called Palestrina, after the village he came from outside Rome. In the 1500s. A man who suffered the death of a brother, two sons and his wife in visitations of the plague.

Later married again; a rich widow, as luck or blessedness would have it. Wrote more than a hundred Masses not to mention motets during his time on earth. Small enough thanks from popes and cardinals and princes. But buried in the end somewhere under the floor of St Peter's Basilica. Exact location no longer known.

Yet leaving to the world the inexhaustible recourse and visionary portal of great music. Granting you, from your first hearing on, an unshaken intuition of something indefinable beyond the veil. Something that *eye hath not seen nor ear heard . . .*

2

Now, much of a lifetime on, you're here in a small parish church across the river from where you live. An ordinary place, as everyday as it can be. But with its own deep story. Was once an abbey. And knew the Black Death also. The mystery is everywhere, and the water deep, although you're far from Palestrina and the Sistine Chapel. And from that transcendent sound. Except when you can link with it these days in cyberspace. In virtual reality, governed by a click.

Here, now, this ordinary, absolute reality. A local funeral. What other kind is there? *Everything is local somewhere.* In this instance the send-off of Amigo Holden of The Hill. Not a close friend, but remembered as a classmate in primary school, out of a class of forty or fifty back in the days.

That cohort of faces thinning out now, one by one. And you yourself feeling the ebb around you and within. Must stay in touch with Larry Stepelevich. Professor Emeritus; philosopher. And his Lithuanian wife, Irene. Those convivial evenings on their house deck in Pennsylvania. A great man for laughter, beers and Hegel, but ambushed like all of us by time; the mounting loss of friends — *Jeeze! They're droppin' through the ice all round me . . .*

3

Amigo Holden lived a mile or more outside the town, up the little road on Fraykawn Hill. A cottage on the edge of woodland. Fond of the drink and old country-and-western songs. The sadder the songs the happier he seemed. After closing time, heading home to his mother while she was still around. Taking a breather now and then along the way. Stopping to relieve himself and sing to everyone and no one. To the sleeping birds maybe. In the dark, looking down on the lights of the town.

The funeral Mass begins this morning with a tinkle of the bell and Emily Linnane singing for the vested entrance of Tom Flannery, the priest. She sings and plays for funerals and weddings, fingering the chords on a tinny-sounding keyboard when she's not too tied up with hairdressing commitments.

Two little girls troop out with the priest, as altar servers. Happy to be let out of school to serve the funeral. Emily usually starts off funeral Masses with *Be not afraid, I go before you always*. Or else *Nearer My God to Thee*. But this time she goes straight for that old Jim Reeves hit that was an even bigger hit in 1964 after the plane he was piloting took a lethal nosedive in Tennessee on the way to Nashville in a blinding storm.

We all rise and a few join in the singing; not unanimous about the key or the words but chancing it anyway.

Adios amigo, adios my friend,
The road we have travelled has come to an end.

Poor old Amigo, says the priest. He says that several times in the course of the ceremony. *Poor old Amigo.* You'd need to be fine-tuned to that expression and its local wavelength. Poor has nothing to do with money, nor old anything to do with age. *Poor old Amigo* in Tom Flannery's mouth carries no condescension. More like compassion. But not that exactly.

Tom can be gruff and cantankerous but people know his form. And that in this life no one gets off scot-free. He's there to help them find some dignity in grief. These days they notice his tendency to limp, the grimace of pain crossing his face. The occasional absentminded hesitation over homily or prayer.

Poor old Amigo. Who can recall Amigo Holden's proper first name, now that he's gone? Joseph, maybe? Or Bartholomew? What was the father's name?

As for the nickname, well, wasn't he a great man for the old Westerns in the Castle Cinema before television took over. Especially the Cisco Kid. And his sidekick Sancho. *South of the Rio Grande. The Gay Amigo. The Girl from San Lorenzo.* Amigo always sat in the back row of the pit. Enchanted in the dark by moving shadows on the screen. Smoking Woodbines sparingly; saving one or two to smoke beside the fire when he got home. And over the years he picked up some Mexican cowboy lingo from the screen. *Hasta la vista. Buenos dias señor. Adios compadre. Por favor amigo.*

4

People line up for Communion as Emily sings again.

Were you there when the stone was rolled away?
Were you there when the stone was rolled away?
Oh sometimes it causes me to tremble, tremble, tremble.
Were you there when the stone was rolled away?

Tributes are paid to Amigo from the altar. Praises he never heard voiced in life. His prowess in his hurling days recounted by someone from the County Board. *A noted exponent of the overhead strike.* Games won or lost or drawn. His loyalty to club and county.

All rise. The two small girls leave the altar steps and stand ready for procession, one bearing the cross. Tom Flannery leads into the final prayers. With incense, holy water, candles. Words of ancient usage, sanctity and grace. That perpetual light may shine on Amigo. That the angels may come to greet him and take him to the bosom of Abraham, and the martyrs come to meet him. That he may know eternal rest where Lazarus is poor no longer.

Men lift together, shoulder out the coffin down the aisle. There are some human tears on human faces. Outside, earth is ready as it always is.

Under this roof a ceremony has been found for Amigo Holden of The Hill. What would Giovanni Pierluigi da Palestrina feel were he to be spirited through centuries to here from his lost grave beneath the great Basilica of Rome? He who lost his brother, wife and two sons to the plague? How might this music fall upon his ear? Emily's choice to play us out. A song Amigo used to sing.

From this valley they say you are going,
We will miss your bright eyes and sweet smile,
For they say you are taking the sunshine
Which has brightened our pathways a while.

LIMERIC
BESIDE B
WED FEB 24th SUN MAR
087 - 6239
CIRCU
FROM MOSCOW WITH LOVE

The Jock

That's street lingo for cancer hereabouts;
veiled monosyllable, both sharp and blunt,
always with the definite article,
a tone of fatalism and pity

for the stricken. It's a generic code
unspoken in consulting room or ward
but traded in the pub or betting shop.
The jock. It's mouthed softly, perhaps

from our spooked image of an unself within
that might stir awake and mount you bareback
to ride out all the way, nor ever spare
the spurs or bridle, bit or riding crop.

Still, some unseat it. Others go on down
with courage like a sanctifying grace.
That trumpet player, longstanding sideman
through all those nights and places, scores and songs —

recall the final evening he contrived
to haul himself upright and eyeball death,
sip at a beer and manage broken breath
enough to sing with you *As Time Goes By*.

The Jupiter Epiphany

Removal time for Florrie, piano woman, songster,
this calm nightfall with fade-up of stars,
feast of Gaspar, Balthazar and Melchior.
She's lifted on men's shoulders at the lit doorway
of the chapel, with a pause for priest to greet
and bless with holy water, as in baptism,
signifying confluence of omega and alpha.

Recall the cadence of the town hall piano,
the temperamental mic, the songs, the nicotine
and brandy timbre of the voice across the years.
Tonight she's all sung out, but in best blouse
and sporting still the rouge, the lipstick and mascara,
the jewelled fingers that set men and women dancing
through their given nights, their orbits of the sun.

All's come down now to elemental word and water,
under great Jupiter, remote yet clear — see
the planetary gleam aligned above the belfry
and envision sarabande of its Galilean moons:
Europa, Ganymede, Io, Callisto . . . in astro time
above a river town, an open door of light,
a woman earthling borne upon men's shoulders.

Florrie is laid before altar, font and crib,
until tomorrow's rituals of otherworld and Earth.
For company tonight she has silence and the dark,
holy family, shepherds, animals and kings —
remembered music is the gift she brings,
those nights the slicked and scented took the floor
for her *Don't Get Around Much Anymore.*

The Other Half

for James and his mother Martina

1

Now that he's grown,
flashback years to
the maternity unit,
the birth of our son.

A nurse invites me to listen in
to the heartbeat in the womb —
its rhythm strong, insistent, amplified
as urgent hoof beats making for
a fateful crossing point,

that prelude soon to merge
with the unheard chorale of all
the living hearts now beating,
beating, beating on in time
with the river in this valley,
and the silent catchment
of all those gone ahead into
the mystery and sweep
of delta and the deep.

2

After that compelling
heart annunciation
from the unborn child
I join wife, nurse and midwife
together in a sanctuary
of birthing and deliverance
where the rhythm deepens

and the trinity of women
is transfigured in my eyes,
shape-shifting to primal
priestess with two acolytes
engrossed in something greater
than themselves or any one of us,
while I am simply getting in their way,
though they say otherwise.

Are you all right, the nurse kept asking me
between the real tasks in hand.
I could have told her
that within my blood
is the embodied shade
of my great-grandmother Mary Ager,
daughter of a shoemaker,
wife of a boatman

dying in the Workhouse ward one February day
in 1881 with ice upon the river
and hunger in the town,
that fourth and final day
of her crucifying labour
at the age of thirty-five —

and how she's come to hold
a haunted niche within my heart,
woman and mother lost and found
whom I might pray to at the hour
of my own death, or this
or any hour of life;

the Workhouse graveyard now
is a small strip of no-man's-land
between housing estates,

all its earned gravity implied
in a weathered plinth and cross
bearing Christ crucified —

young children in the flowering
innocence of summer
adopt it as a playground
that they call
the place where Jesus is buried.

3

These women here and now
are not concerned
with burial or death
but with a living infant
heading towards the light —

they lean into the work
of now and its necessity,
the ageless rite of birthing
we call labour, as in toil —

contractions, respirations,
anguished cries
Oh Jesus! Jesus Christ!
urgings and assurances and pain.

Push! Push! Breathe in!
Breathe in and push again!
Good girl! Good girl! Relax a while! —
all the messy, incarnate business
of a human being
being born

while I'm an incidental extra
cast as *emotional support*,
a redundant interloper
feeling oddly alien or other.

4

So the women's work goes on
until the heart-shaken
climax that is fruit
of all this toil,
that mortally immortal
crossing point in time —

the suddenly eruptive
emergence of the child
into our sight,
under the raw reality
of light.

With that first shock of seeing,
of first breath
and fragile cry,
my vision blurs to tears

while the midwife raises up
and then hands on the infant,
already flexing limbs,
to my exhausted wife, announcing,
A little man, God bless him!
Then to me, *are you all right?*

I still swim out of focus,
out of time, as naked

and unknowing as the child.
Who are these strange beings
bringing this to pass?
Where do they come from?

I'm fine, I mumble, bending
to kiss the mother,
wipe her brow,
behold our son.
My tears fall on her face
and on the child.

Who am I and who is she? —
each of us embodying
both *animus* and *anima*,
mutually singular
while singularly dual.

What are we doing here?
And who is, was, will be
this newborn child
now given to the world?
I weigh within my hand
the tiny feet on which he'll stand
to make his way and walk
whatever paths he'll find.

May he be blessed
and bless in turn.
These are the feet.
This is the world.

5

The midwife calls a doctor —
some routine repair work
to be done. She comes breezing in,
a young Canadian, a brunette,
immaculate in white, attractive
(it doesn't go away despite
the blood and sweat and cries —
that erotic gravity
that makes it all begin
and gives the world its spin).

Hi! No problems here, right?
she briskly greets us, appraises,
slipping on surgical gloves
to sponge some blood aside,
see to the intimate
needlework required.

Invisible mending done,
she straightens up,
dark mane tossed back,
and stretches, spreading
her arms wide to add
Congratulations all! — then smiles,
washes her hands and slips out
to another call, asking as she brushes
past my shoulder and away,
are you okay?

I'm still in shock, still peering through
the mist of my unknowing,
although my heart surgeon's told me

that the hearts of men and women
are freely interchangeable

I've found myself to be
a kind of outside agent here
who has witnessed face-to-face
woman's death-defying miracle
that remains apart and ageless

but is still a primal sharing
and a carnal consecration
of humankind's heart song,
whereby all of our duality
is subsumed and reborn.

The Garden and the Scattering

Again the time has come for you
to call me from my book
and help put order
on the fallen leaves.

Before we can consign them
to bags or compost bin
there is the raking and sweeping
into heaps, an orderly array

which even as we pause for breath
becomes again an agitated
plaything of the wind that wilfully
comes calling from the river.

How mundane yet strange
this suburban ritual we share
with the darkening days,
a rite which you initiate each year

as though instinctively
to join a dance
of sweepers
and the swept

tuned to the absolute
embrace of days
beyond all of our
imagining or ways.

Walking the Ground

And so last year
in damp October weather
I joined the three-hour tour with
Beatrice, our guide, a Polish actress,
mother and historian,
on this working day
she's rostered to enunciate
her unflawed English narrative
of a domain beyond words,

leading with as much
self-imposed detachment
as she can for her own good
on a long trail through
the circles and the stagings
of what had been an earthly
purgatorio and hell
of lives beyond recounting
that leave us dumb.

Yet this day of my life
has come when I,
if only for a day
in this unforgiven place,
might take and deconstruct
the word holiday as holy
with a pilgrim gesture of intent
to assuage by going there
and walking the ground
a token grain
of immeasurable wrong
that can never be undone,

for how else can we weigh
and recognize the good

other than by looking
the dark mystery
of evil in the face — its real
presence in the world,
its dark seeding
that can propagate
by any river,
find footing
in any soil?

Though last year has gone
and wild flowers show spring faces
between ruins and railway lines
of Auschwitz-Birkenau
they don't silence
the haunting and unreasoned
self-interrogation
that entered me that day
and which I bore home
in my soul:

in those years of atrocity
by the confluence
of Vistula and Sola
while I was still learning
my first prayers and songs
beside the Suir —

had I been of age
and to the east
of my known world
as prisoner, slave labourer,
as *Kapo*, jailor, officer
or looker-on —
what might I
have known and done
of right or wrong?

A Joyful Haunting

In my early teens the Chris Barber Jazz Band came to Carrick-on-Suir, decanting themselves from a couple of cars to play for a dance at the local Ormond Hall. I have no idea what brought them there from London to our small Irish town. My parents smuggled me in past the box office to hear the music and meet the band since I was struggling to learn trombone and discovering the music of New Orleans and beyond.

I've never forgotten that October night in 1955. For the first time ever I was hearing real jazz in the flesh and it touched some core part of me. By the time I came to do my Leaving Cert I was listening to Louis Armstrong, Miles Davis and Duke Ellington while my classmates were hung up on Bill Haley and someone called Elvis Presley ... And soon I'd be discovering the visionary Seán Ó Riada who had jazz leanings and would revolutionize the Irish traditional musical scene. Over the coming years my musical tastes would become broadly eclectic, embracing classical and Irish traditional genres as well as jazz of various eras.

But that magic night when I first heard and met the Chris Barber band in our now vanished dancehall haunts me still, and it's a haunting of delight. The front line of trumpet, trombone and clarinet was backed by banjo, bass and drums. Together in full flight they could jump for joy. That's what that improvisatory music proclaimed — the sheer sensuous joy of being alive in the now ...

Along with the band there was also a young blues singer from County Down. Her name was Ottilie Patterson, then aged 23, daughter of an Irish father and a Latvian mother. Ottilie, an art student, had recently joined the Barber band. I was a very shy schoolboy beside the bandstand but she chatted with me between sets.

So also did Chris Barber the trombone player when I was introduced to him during a break. The mild-mannered Chris was the son of a statistician father and a headmistress mother. He had studied at the Guildhall School of Music and would become and remain a major figure in British jazz. As I write a lifetime on he's still blowing the trombone and touring, while the other original sidemen are no longer in the world. When I was presented to him on that long-ago night as a schoolboy learner on trombone his immediate advice was to find myself a good teacher. Had that option been available to me who knows how it might have changed my life and its direction? I still describe myself as a 'lapsed' trombone player, with the door not finally shut on the possibility of being born again if someone out there could fix my faulty embouchure...

On the night I first met and heard the Barber band they were on the way to becoming a big jazz name in Britain and beyond it. The clarinet player, Monty Sunshine, would have a major hit with *Petite Fleur*, written by Sidney Bechet of New Orleans and later Paris. The banjo player in the back of the band, Lonnie Donegan, would have a huge transatlantic success with his version of *Rock Island Line* during the skiffle craze. Pat Halcox, the trumpet lead from Chelsea, had set out to be a research chemist until he found his true vocation. Solid as a rock, he'd be blowing jazz with Barber for the next fifty years.

And here they were in full cry, those musicians — all of them then young, I now realize — filling the dancehall in our town with the sounds of joy, a hall that would in a short few years be demolished to make way for a supermarket where sometimes I pause now in the aisles and strain to hear those haunting echoes out of time.

A few months before that night in 1955 the Barber band had participated in a concert at the Royal Festival Hall that would prove to be a musical milestone. Some of it was recorded. I saved up for and still have the well-worn vinyl EP on which Ottilie Patterson sings *St Louis Blues* on her first big public appearance in a major London venue. She was from the little village of Comber, County Down, and grew up with piano lessons and some scratchy old Bessie Smith records. She'd be married to Chris Barber for some years and on US tours earn the admiration of such grounded American bluesmen as Big Bill Broonzy, Muddy Waters, Sonny Terry and Brownie McGee.

In later years she'd develop some problems with her voice and eventually have to retire from fulltime singing. She moved to Scotland and lived there in semi-obscurity until she died in Ayr on the 20th of June 2011, aged 79. There was a private family funeral back home in Comber and she was buried in the family plot. Obituaries were published in Britain and in Belfast but I saw no media attention paid south of the border.

One of these days perhaps I may shape a symmetry of meeting and of memory, heading north to stand by Ottilie Patterson's resting place in County Down, bridging the span of time and change since 1955. Music can outflank time and its attrition. I reach back as I write, recall a shy schoolboy beside the dancehall stage on a night long gone, and a young woman in a party dress, stepping up in front of the band to sing of love and loss in tones of passionate proclaiming. *I hate to see the evenin' sun go down . . .*

Where or When

for Anne and Harry Doherty

Two men, old friends, musicians,
walk the tow-path by the river
retracing nights and places,
sidemen and songs,
the tempo of the years,
the right notes and the wrong.

The wife of one, who sang those nights
along with them, is old and ill.
The men pretend that they
may still ignore
time's undertow —

she's past that foolishness,
but wasn't she a beauty
in her day
and in her nights?

She had a glow and that's for sure.
And she could sing . . .

Like old men everywhere
they ask themselves where now
are songs like those
they still recall from times
of peace or war?

Life was not romantic
then or ever,
except when retold
in poetry or song.

They pause
where the river slows
to a dark pool
before they turn for home.

No one else is near.

As dusk draws in
they start to hum
a Rodgers and Hart tune
from long ago and far away,

sharing implied chord changes,
exchanging half-forgotten
words and phrases, conjuring
between the lines and spaces

the heart of loss
that lies beyond the notes,
the singing
and the song.

Can they be heard
beyond the river bend?

It seems we stood and talked like this before,
we looked at each other in the same way then
but I can't remember where or when...

Where There Was None

for Martina

She's made a garden.

In her own time
in her own way

air and water
seed and clay

spring by summer
year by day

dark by light
and hope by hands

cold by wet
and sun by faith

here where there
was none before

in her own time
in her own way

she's made a garden.

Changelings

in the National Library

Yeats was inclined to exhibit himself
in public or private, mainly in London,
away with the fairies or Cuchulainn,
Madame Blavatsky and Maud Gonne,
Celtic Twilight and Golden Dawn.

He might have been a man more grounded,
but had he been, then perhaps my father
on lost evenings of my boyhood
might not have had 'The Stolen Child'
to say by heart from his sickbed, nor ever

have become that shade that waylays me
here in the National Library of Ireland,
his faint voice reaching across the years,
intimately telling his eldest child
of otherworld, enchantment, tears.

On the Eve of a Tree-felling

*The trees are coming into leaf
Like something almost being said . . .*
　　　　　　　　　　　— Philip Larkin

I reach out for your hand between the sheets. A bit like a first night, or like a last. All is calm outside the window. Earth keeping its own counsel. It's late. Or early. Though not too late for change of mind or heart. Insinuating whisper of the leaves, the living branches just outside. Is it possible that trees may have their own way of knowing?

We've talked it through, or so we think. The silence between us is intimately eloquent. We've finally decided to end the life of the tree we planted there beside the house some forty years ago.

There was a time when man did not so dictate the fate of trees. In upper New York state there is a forest in which nature is allowed to shape things as it may; as an arboreal experiment. As though no man had ever yet set foot in that place. Just as it was here on our island after the ice had gone and trees had clothed the valleys and the hills. Before first campfire and smoke of settlement.

There are ghost trees and forests of the past now everywhere invisible. Where now stand cathedrals, great concert halls, parliaments, hospitals, museums, castles, skyscrapers, highways, houses, towns and cities. Imagine countless trees inhabiting such spaces, along with animals and birdsong and no people for ages yet to come.

We've talked it through. Postponed and vacillated. Remembered the tree outside the window growing along with our lives and our children's lives through nights and days and years. *Our* tree. The assumptive arrogance of that. *Our* silver birch, *betula pendula*, lady of the woods. Its leafing and unleafing. Its flourishing.

Storms it managed to outlive. The terrible night in 1979 of unexpected August hurricane and Fastnet Rock yacht race disaster. Wild winds raging through Munster. Beating against our bedroom window far inland while we clung to one another in the dark as boats were foundering in fifty-foot waves; expert sailors drowning miles out in the maelstrom.

Our stripling tree was scarred that night but bent meekly before the storm; held out, grew on beside us.

There's still time left for reprieve though the appointed executioners will be at the door with chainsaws, climbing-gear and shredder by eight o'clock. There are reasons for felling. *Sensible* reasons — whatever that word *sensible* may mean. Safety. Responsibility. Unforeseen size, closeness to the house, possible decay, storms, acts of God. Consideration for the neighbours' share of light and shade. Some people go in fear of trees or overhanging branches. Reasons and boundaries. And reasons for reasons.

And for not felling? Unreason. Love. Beauty. Life and custom. The bonds and branching of shared living, of memory and attachment. We have consulted with our close friend and advisor, Pádraig; tree lover and planter, devoted gardener, scholar and wit, now gone to ground. The many times we called upon his counselling and balance.

Of course after all the for and against we must remember that in the end all trees die too, however much we love them. They go, one way or another. Just like ourselves and everything we know. Even the stars and planets. There comes a time in the affairs of men and trees . . .

It's late. Or early. Although not yet past time for change of mind or heart. Our silence is a kind of sighing, both of love and sorrow. As we lie here wordless in the dark does each of us still hope for a sign from the other? A sign of dissent, a sign of resignation or reprieve?

And so I have reached out in uncertainty to take your hand between the sheets. A bit like a first night, or like a last.

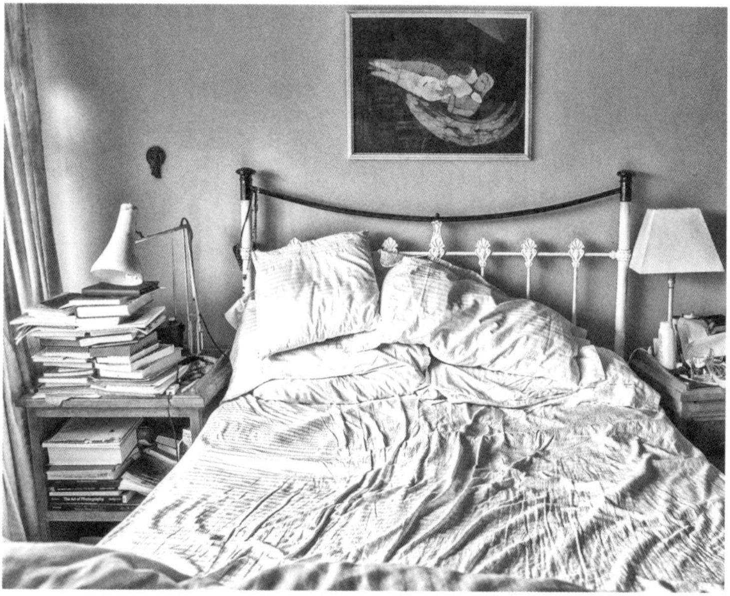

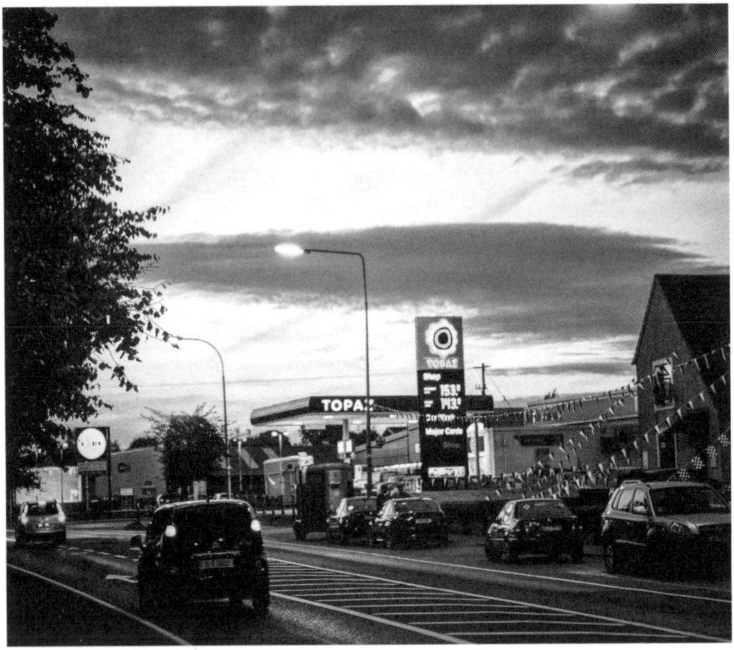
TOPAZ
Shop
Major Cards

Benediction on the Sixteenth Day of May

Life is once, forever.
— Henri Cartier-Bresson

Blessèd be his bad heart which allows him leave
to rest in sunshine on a broken chair
on this feast day of Brendan, voyager.
Close by, his wife is on her knees
in her allotment,
attending to her planting,
her strawberries and aubergines,
her broccoli and beans and weeds,
here in the former convent grounds
beside the river,

and blessèd be that river,
sister river of three sisters,
its weirsong and its ancient bridge,
and blessèd too be Clareen Well behind him,
the fire station and the main road to Clonmel,
to all points west and back,
with all its human traffic
and its transience.

Birds on every side sound out their manifestos,
yea, even rooks and jackdaws rasping out
staccato climax of their *sacre du printemps*.
We're part of some great symphony,
he thinks to tell his wife, but leaves
the obvious unsaid since they both seem
so tuned and yet so different
within this place and time.
Blessèd be not saying
when there's no need to say.

He begins to feel these days
the weight of all the times
he's been around the star that energizes
all of this, begins to wonder at how life
and time have taught him
less and less of certainty —
though in some deeper way.
He recalls his mother musing
towards the end,
Do I remember this or did I dream it?

What matter either way?
The winter past was one of stormy
nights and days that brought their share
of last processions touching on their lives —
neighbour, friend, acquaintance followed
by the walking living and the wounded,
heads bent against the weather
as they crossed the bridge, the river,
to the boneyard on the hill.
Blessèd be the boneyard
and the bent heads that live on.

He looks up to the east;
the town-clock tower above West Gate,
the sun-warmed salmon and the bell
that soon will strike out 4
this Maytime afternoon.

Hear a key change in the river
as the current slows, responding to recycled
motif in the eternal triangle, the dance
of sun and moon and earth —

a new floodtide surprises, slipping in,
taking time to probe, lay siege
and rise until weirsong is muted
and then overcome
once again by tidal swell.

Blessèd be the broken
chair he rests upon.
Blessèd be the woman
kneeling on the earth.
Blessèd be the stillness
as the river holds its breath.

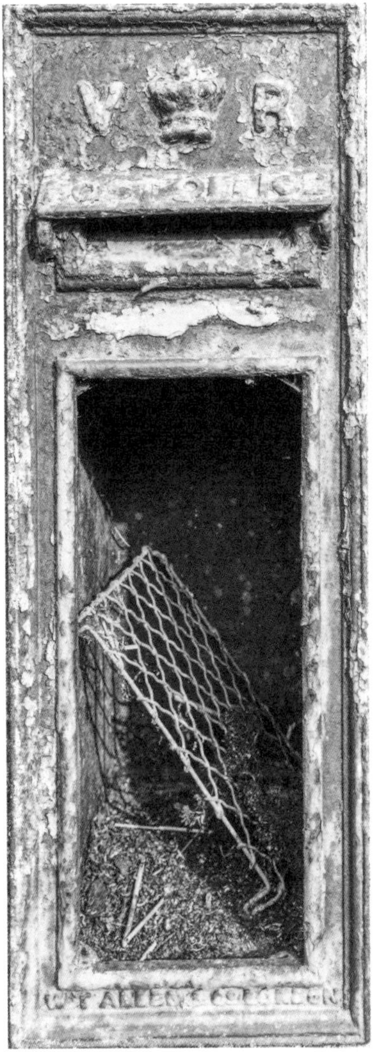
V R
ALLEN

Notes and Acknowledgements

page 19 *spéirbhean*: literally 'sky-woman'; a beautiful woman/ apparition, often symbolizing Ireland, in the set Gaelic genre of *aisling* or vision poem of the 17-18th centuries.
ceo draíochta: magic mist
page 20 *Sruthán*: stream
page 21 *uaigneas*: loneliness, aloneness, desolation
page 34 *saoi*: literally 'wise one', also the highest honour for members of Aosdána.
page 37 *Sláinte na mbeo is na marbh*: '[Here's a] health to the living and the dead.'
page 43 photograph of the late Joseph ('the Joker') Griffin who habitually speculated on the universe and existence from his vantage point of Tullahought in south Kilkenny.

Thanks are due to the editors/producers of the following publications and radio features in which some of these poems and prose pieces, or versions of them, first appeared or were broadcast: *1916: Ireland in Contemporary Art*, touring exhibition curated by Larry Lambe, *An Experiment in Social Embroidery*, ed. Theresia Guschlbauer, Clonmel Junction Festival; *Berryman's Fate*, ed. Philip Coleman, Arlen House; *Clifden Anthology*, eds. Joseph Woods, Brendan Flynn; *Connemara & Aran*, Walter Pfeiffer, Artisan House Editions; *Forty: Gallery Press 40th anniversary celebration*, Abbey Theatre; *Irish Pages*, ed. Chris Agee; *Peter Fallon: Poet, Publisher, Translator, Editor*, ed. Richard Rankin Russell, Irish Academic Press; *Poetry Ireland Review*, eds. John F Deane, Vona Groarke; *Sunday Miscellany* RTE Radio, producer Cliodhna Ní Anluain; *The Enchanted Verses*, Indian journal, Irish issue, ed. Patrick Cotter; *The Irish Times*, Poetry Editor Gerard Smyth; *The Stony Thursday Book*, ed. Peter Sirr; *Windows 20 anthology*, eds. Heather Brett & Noel Monahan.

'A State of Light' was commissioned by Clifden Arts Festival and set to music for soprano voice and string quartet by Bill

Whelan. It was first performed in association with Ballynahinch Castle Hotel, Connemara, by Deirdre Moynihan, soprano, and the Kaleidoscope ensemble, at the Station House Theatre, Clifden, on 26 September 2013 and repeated the following evening at UCC. A further performance of the work was given by the RTE ConTempo Quartet, with Deirdre Moynihan, at the Hugh Lane Gallery, Dublin, on 31 May 2015.

I express my gratitude for residencies at the remarkable Clifden Arts Festival and also acknowledge the support of The Arts Council/An Chomhairle Ealaíon in the publication of this book, along with personal support through my membership of Aosdána. The encouragement of my wife Martina and our family is something for which I am thankful; so is the vibrant and sustaining community and place into which I was born and where I continue to live. Finally I must restate how fortunate I am to be published to the consistent standard of excellence associated, nationally and internationally, with The Gallery Press under its founder and editor, the poet Peter Fallon.